2016

Merry Christmas
Blythe!

Love,
Uncle Mike, Aunt Carrie,
Josh, Sam & Owen

To Paula Wiseman,
who somehow always knows.
—D. J. N.

For my mother, Emily.
And to all of those in the world
who plant the seeds of change.
—K. N.

ACKNOWLEDGMENTS

The author thanks her family, John Mugane, Njoroge Ngari
Mukarara, Anne Ngugi, Esther Nyaga, Richard Tchen,
and, most of all, Paula Wiseman, without whom this
book would never have existed.

SIMON & SCHUSTER BOOKS FOR YOUNG READERS · An imprint of Simon & Schuster Children's Publishing Division · 1230 Avenue of the Americas, New York, New York 10020 · Text copyright © 2010 by Donna Jo Napoli · Illustrations copyright © 2010 by Kadir Nelson, Inc. · All rights reserved, including the right of reproduction in whole or in part in any form. · SIMON & SCHUSTER BOOKS FOR YOUNG READERS is a trademark of Simon & Schuster, Inc. · For information about special discounts for bulk purchases, please contact Simon & Schuster Special Sales at 1-866-506-1949 or business @simonandschuster.com. · The Simon & Schuster Speakers Bureau can bring authors to your live event. For more information or to book an event, contact the Simon & Schuster Speakers Bureau at 1-866-248-3049 or visit our website at www.simonspeakers.com. · Book design by Lizzy Bromley · The text for this book is set in Manticore and Allison. · Manufactured in China · 0716 SCP · 8 10 9 7   · Library of Congress Cataloging-in-Publication Data · Napoli, Donna Jo, 1948– · Mama Miti: Wangari Maathai and the trees of Kenya / Donna Jo Napoli ; Illustrated by Kadir Nelson. · p. cm. · Includes bibliographical references. · ISBN 978-1-4169-3505-6 (hardcover : alk. paper) · 1. Maathai, Wangari—Juvenile literature. 2. Tree planters (Persons)—Kenya—Biography—Juvenile literature. 3. Women conservationists—Kenya—Biography—Juvenile literature. 4. Green Belt Movement (Society : Kenya)—Juvenile literature. I. Nelson, Kadir, ill. II. Title. · SB63.M22N37 2010 · 333.72092—dc22 · [B] · 2008023604

MAMA MITI

Wangari Maathai and the Trees of Kenya

Written by
Donna Jo Napoli

Illustrated by
Kadir Nelson

A Paula Wiseman Book
Simon & Schuster Books for Young Readers
New York London Toronto Sydney

On the highlands of Africa,
near forests and plains and a huge salt lick,
Wangari was born. The face of
Mount Kenya smiled down on her.
People told stories of how in the old days
sometimes the sun shone too bright too long,
and droughts came. Creatures suffered.
Plants wilted. People fought.
So the men held ceremonies under the
mugumo—the spreading sacred fig tree—
and the skies blessed them with shimmering
rains to slake their thirst and water their farms.
Village elders placed staffs from the
thigi tree between angry men,
and enemies became friends.

WANGARI LISTENED TO THESE STORIES.
That's how she came to love and respect trees.
That's how she came to be wise in the tradition
of her family and village, of her country and
continent.

When Wangari grew up, she worked in the city, but she always remembered her roots. She planted trees in her backyard and sat under them to refresh her body and spirit.

One day a poor woman came from the western valley to see the wise Wangari. Her children peeked out from behind her at the smiling woman in bright blue cloth with squiggles all through it, like tadpoles squirming in a pool. "I have too little food to feed my family," said the poor woman. "There is no longer a job for me in the timber mill. And I have no other skills. What can I do?"

Wangari took the woman's hands and turned them over. She took the children's hands, one by one. "These are strong hands. Here are seedlings of the *mubiru muiru* tree. Plant them. Plant as many as you can. Eat the berries."

Thayu nyumba—
Peace, my people

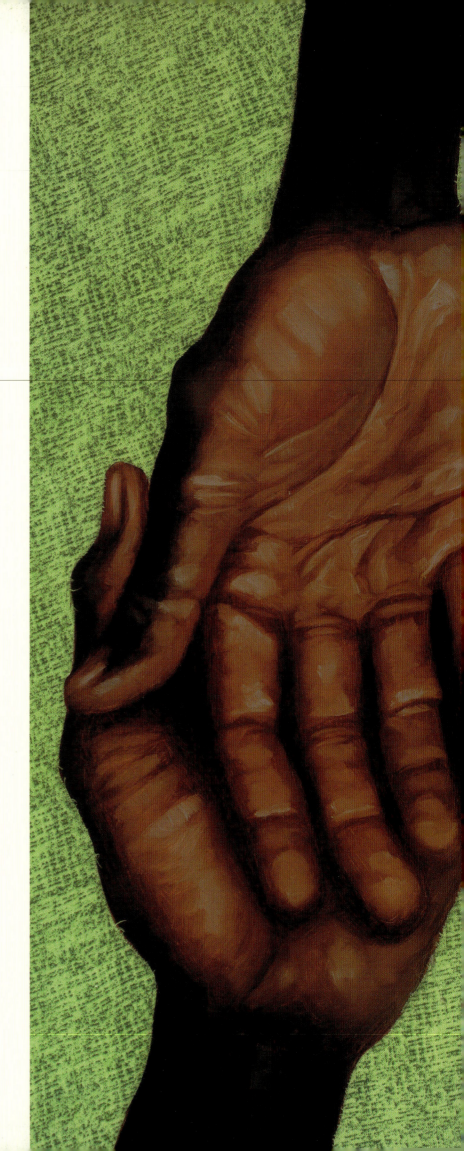

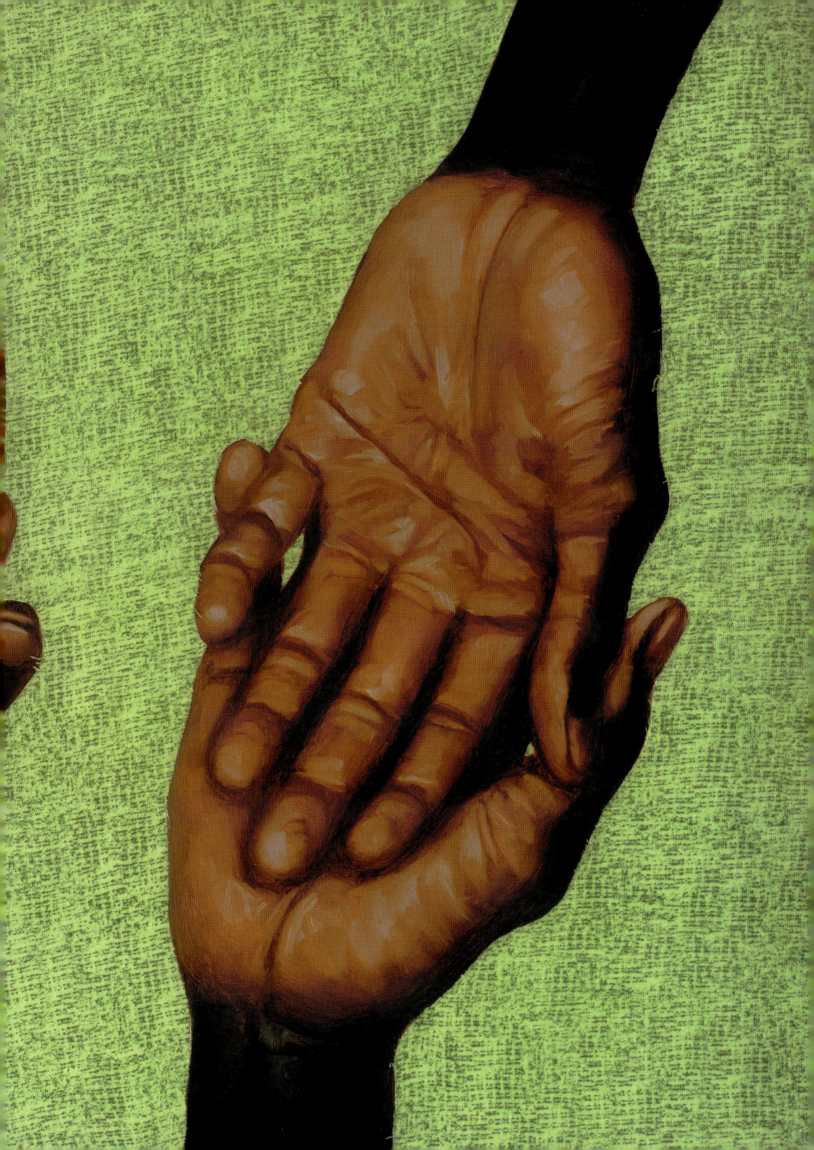

The woman and her children returned home and planted trees with their strong hands, one by one. In the years to come, when flowering season was over, the family ate the shiny round fruits. They shared with their neighbors, who carried home the seeds, planted them, and grew their own *mubiru muiru* trees.

Another woman came to the wise Wangari, as poor as the first. This one traveled from the mountain in the south. Her daughters stood beside her, thin as ropes. "My daughters and I walk hours every day to find firewood to cook with," said the poor woman. "It takes so long, we have no time for anything else. What can I do?"

Wangari took the woman by the arms. "These arms are strong," she said. "Plant a tree. Here are seedlings of the *mukinduri*. This tree makes good firewood. Plant as many as you can."

Thayu nyumba—
Peace, my people

The woman and her daughters planted those seedlings. In time the trees grew huge with many wide branches. The woman and her daughters cut branches for warmth. They shared new seedlings with their neighbors, who carried them home and grew their own *mukinduri* trees.

Word passed from woman to woman, until all over Kenya women knew about the wise Wangari. They came to her from every direction, one after another, as the years went by.

"Our goats are starving," said a woman from near the northern desert. "I have barely enough food to feed my family; how can my husband feed the animals, too?"

"Plant a tree. A *muheregendi*. The leaves are good animal fodder. Plant as many as you can."

Thayu nyumba— Peace, my people

"My cows are sick," said another, from the savanna. "I have no money to buy medicine for them."

"Plant a tree. A *muthakwa wa athi*. The leaves cure gall sickness in cattle."

Thayu nyumba— Peace, my people

"Wild animals come in the night and steal my chickens," said a woman from a fishing village. She shook her head in worry.

"Plant a tree. A *mukawa*. Its thorns will keep out predators."

Thayu nyumba— Peace, my people

"My home fell apart" came the cry of another woman, who had come all the way from the coast. "We have no shelter."

"Plant a tree. A *muluhakuha*. The timber makes good building poles."

Thayu nyumba— Peace, my people

Wangari told women to plant *murigono*, whose branches make good stakes for training yam vines.

She told them to plant *muhuti* as a living fence around their animal yards.

She told them to plant *muigoya*, whose leaves could be wrapped around bananas to ripen them.

She told them to plant *muringa* for the pure joy of their white flowers.

And when a woman from her own village came, lamenting that the water in her stream was too dirty to drink, Wangari told her to plant *mukuyu*, the giant sacred fig, the drinker of water, which acts as nature's filter to clean streams.

Thayu nyumba—
Peace, my people

Soon cool, clear waters teemed with black wriggling tadpoles, like the ones on Wangari's clothes—like the ones Wangari marveled at in the waters when she was small, when Kenya was covered with trees and animals, when people lived in peace with nature.

All over the countryside the trees that had disappeared came back. Nairobi, the capital city, had been known as Kiinuini, "the place where there are many miiinu trees." Now it was Kiinuini again. Kenya was strong once more, strong and peaceful.

Wangari changed a country, tree by tree. She taught her people the ancient wisdom of peace with nature. And now she is teaching the rest of the world. She is known these days as Mama Miti—the mother of trees. A green belt of peace started with one good woman offering something we can all do: "Plant a tree."

Thayu nyumba—
Peace, my people

Afterword

Wangari Muta Maathai was the first African woman to win the Nobel Peace Prize. That was in 2004. That was one of her many amazing firsts.

Wangari was born on April 1, 1940, in Nyeri, Kenya. At that time girls from rural Kenya rarely received an education. But Wangari studied in the United States and in Germany. When she returned to Kenya, she worked in veterinary medicine at the University of Nairobi and became the first woman in central or eastern Africa to earn a PhD. She taught at the university and eventually became the head of the veterinary medicine faculty, another first: No woman had headed any department at any university in Kenya before.

Wangari Maathai's study of animals and nature made her a leader in the fields of ecology, sustainable development, natural resources, and wildlife. In 1976, while working for the National Council of Women of Kenya, she started the Green Belt Movement, a national grassroots organization to combat deforestation of Kenya. Through the years she courageously and consistently argued for peaceful coexistence of people and nature, often battling political and economic powers that stood to gain financially from cutting down the trees. Her work for the environment landed her in prison in 1991, but she was freed due to an Amnesty International letter-writing campaign. She's been arrested many times since then for her steady campaign for peace, but no one has been able to stop her. In 2002 the people of Kenya elected her to their parliament. Two years later she was awarded the Nobel Peace Prize.

In 1976 Wangari Maathai introduced the idea of planting trees for peace to Kenyan citizens. Since then, the Green Belt Movement has planted more than thirty million trees in Kenya and in other countries of Africa. The trees prevent soil erosion, filter water and air, and provide firewood and food and timber for shelters. The work is done primarily by village women, who are reclaiming their rights and responsibilities as keepers of the earth and caretakers of its future. But men now help too.

Wangari Maathai's work is the embodiment of the Kenyan notion of *harambee*—the spirit of pulling together for the common good.

Thayu nyumba—Peace, my people.

Kikuyu Glossary

harambee: the spirit of pulling together for the common good. (This is actually a Swahili word.)

Kiinuini: the place where there are many cassia trees, now called Nairobi.

mama miti: mother of trees.

miinu: a cassia tree. (Scientific name: CASSIA DIDYMOBOTRYA.)

mubiru muiru: a small tree with edible berries. (Scientific name: VANGUERIA LINEARISEPALA.)

mugumo: a fig tree that is sacred to the Kikuyu people, the most populous ethnic group of Kenya. (Scientific name: FICUS THONNINGII.)

muheregendi: a tree in the linden family that makes good animal fodder. (Scientific name: GREWIA SIMILIS.)

muhuti: a tree used to make cattle enclosures. (Scientific name: ERYTHRINA ABYSSINICA.)

muigoya: a plant that can grow into a thick hedge, whose leaves are used for ripening bananas.
   (Scientific name: PLECTRANTHUS BARBATUS.)

mukawa: a thorny bush with edible berries. (Scientific name: CARISSA EDULIS.)

mukinduri: a tall forest tree that makes good firewood. (Scientific name: CROTON MEGALOCARPUS.)

mukuyu: a sycamore fig tree that is believed to filter water better than other trees. (Scientific name: FICUS SYCOMORUS.)

muluhakuha: a tall straight tree used for poles. (Scientific name: MACARANGA KILIMANDSCHARICA.)

murigono: a shrub that makes a good animal enclosure; also used for stakes for training yam vines.
   (Scientific name: CLERODENDRUM JOHNSTONII.)

muringa: a large tree cut for timber, covered with white flowers. (Scientific name: CORDIA AFRICANA.)

muthakwa wa athi: a shrub whose leaves can cure cattle gall. (Scientific name: CRASSOCEPHALUM MANNII.)

thayu nyumba: a phrase for wishing calm upon everyone's home, translated here as "peace, my people."

thigi: the "peace" tree of Kenya. It's actually more of a bush, and village elders placed staffs made of it between
   fighters to help them reconcile. (Scientific name: LANNEA SCHWEINFURTHII var. STUHLMANNII.)

A Note from the Author

As I did the research for this story, I surrounded myself with books about Kenya that had photographs of the people and the country. I also looked in many botany books for information about particular trees.

Many books provided information about Wangari Maathai and about the Green Belt Movement, including Wangari's own *Unbowed: A Memoir* (New York: Knopf, 2006) and *The Green Belt Movement: Sharing the Approach and the Experience* (New York: Lantern Books, 2004) as well as *The Two Faces of Civil Society: NGOs and Politics in Africa*, by Stephen N. Ndegwa (West Hartford, CT: Kumarian Press, 1996), and *A Rising Public Voice: Women in Politics Worldwide*, edited by Alida Brill (New York: Feminist Press at CUNY, 1995).

Other books helped by providing general information about the social situation of women and the economic effects that women are having on the country of Kenya today, such as *Gender and Economic Growth in Kenya: Unleashing the Power of Women*, by Amanda Ellis, Jozefina Cutura, Nouma Dione, Ian Gillson, Clare Manuel, and Judy Thongori (Washington, DC: World Bank, 2007); *Women in Kenya: Repression and Resistance* (New York: Amnesty International, 1995); *Gender, Environment, and Development in Kenya: A Grassroots Perspective*, by Barbara P. Thomas-Slayter, Dianne E. Rocheleau, Isabella Asamba, Mohamud Jama, Charity Kabutha, Njoki Mbuthi, Elizabeth Oduor-Noah, Karen Schofield-Leca, Betty Wamalwa-Muragori, and Leah Wanjama (Boulder, CO: Lynne Rienner, 1995); *Unveiling Women as Pillars of Peace: Peace Building in Communities Fractured by Conflict in Kenya: An Interim Report*, by Monica Kathina Juma (New York: United Nations Development Programme, 2000); and *Kenya: The Role of Women in Economic Development* (Washington, DC: World Bank, 1989).

Internet sources were wonderful, especially those that included interviews with Wangari Maathai. In particular, I found these very useful:

The Greenbelt Movement
http://greenbeltmovement.org/index.php

Nobelprize.org, Wangari Maathai Nobel Lecture
http://nobelprize.org/nobel_prizes/peace/laureates/2004/maathai-lecture.html

Nobelprize.org, Wangari Maathai Biography
http://nobelprize.org/nobel_prizes/peace/laureates/2004/maathai-bio.html

FAO Corporate Document Repository, Social and Economic Incentives for Smallholder Tree Growing, Chapter 2
http://www.fao.org/docrep/u8995e/u8995e0b.htm

Nature Kenya
http://www.naturekenya.org/index.html

I also used a website that is no longer on the Web, but which I accessed on July 25, 2006, at http://www.restore-earth .org/brackenhurst.htm.

A Note from the Illustrator

The artwork is rendered with oil paints and printed fabrics on gessoed board. I chose to use these materials because African culture is rich with textiles and color, and I felt it essential that the artwork reflect an aesthetic of both East Africa and my own work. It was a bit of a challenge telling this story using mostly fabric and so little paint, but rewarding nonetheless. I hope I've been able to capture the spirit and culture of Kenya, Wangari Maathai, and the Green Belt Movement.